Black Coffee
No Sugar No Cream

By: Crystal White

First published by AuthorHouse 04/08/04

ISBN: 1-4140-8024-7 (e-book)
ISBN: 1-4184-2608-3 (Paperback)

Printed in the United States of America
Bloomington, Indiana

This book is printed on acid free paper.

Dedication

This book is dedicated in loving memory of my beloved Aunt Meal. Words can not truly express how I feel. I know that I miss you more and more every single day but I take comfort in knowing that you are looking down upon me smiling.
For Michey. Girl, you have been there through thick and thin. I love u for life and that will never change.
For all others who believed...

Table Of Contents

Frankie

As a child u grow up thinking you're invincible
U have your life mapped out and u know exactly where you're going and
who you're gonna be
When u get older u think back and laugh cuz life never quite happens the
way u want it to
But I will alwayz remember Christmases and Spring Breaks and just about
every other holiday or time off
When Uncle Frank would pack the family in the minivan and u guys
would head down to Arkansas
We couldn't wait til u all got there cuz we all knew what that meant
Hiding-go-seek in the dark when we stayed on Crystal Hill
Long nites spent laughing and pickin on Jarvis and crackin jokes on each
other
Riding bikes and playing football and getting yelled at by Aunt Ora
Remember Jewell was the Mother Hen that tried to keep us all in line
But with u and Alton around we were alwayz in some kind of trouble
As we got older the visits grew further apart
But no matter how old we got there was alwayz a sense of excitement
when "Uncle Frank's kids" came down
We knew u were gonna make us laugh with your off-the-wall stories and
your crazy comments
I will never forget last Thanksgiving when we hung out
We talked and laughed about old times
And I took u on base and u asked me a million and one questions about the
Army
And on the way back we shared those sweet and sour things that u like
(Well, u pretty much ate them up from me)
But I'll still remember it
So it's hard to believe that you've left us
Keep smiling
And alwayz remember that we love u, Frankie

In Love With U

I've come to the conclusion
That you've come to the conclusion
That u could actually be with me
If only there weren't so many people around
Looking us up and down
But…man…I don't care about them
And what I once thought was a fantasy
Is slowly becoming reality
I see it…like I see your beautiful face in my sleep
I've fallen in love with u over and over again
Until sometimes it just hurts
I want u to be a part of my world
Because I feel that u would love it here
If only I didn't love u so much then it wouldn't hurt so much
But don't u want somebody to love u
Cuz I truly do; if only I had more time I could tell u why
If only I had more words I'd have more rhyme
Your beauty can't be defined and neither can these feelings I've been
trying to hide
If u weren't so…weren't so…u I wouldn't have these feelings
So it's all your fault
Make me stop these thoughts
Cuz what's worse than not having u is losing u
And…I don't want to lose u
But I can't afford to keep silent
It's violent
The way you're killin me softly…
And the way I don't mind
You're not a dime
But that gold piece that I would proudly show off to spectators
But if I can't have u
The next person has to
Love u half as much as I do
I wish I were in their shoes
So I could step to u

But all I have is this poem
And even this isn't good enuff
The only thing I can give u
Is all that I have
I won't promise u the moon and the stars
Cuz they aren't mine
But I will promise u my love, my heart, my time
For that's all I have; all for u
I guess this is my fantasy not yours
So I should quit trying to incorporate u into my dreams
It just gets crazy sometimes when I can't get u out of my mind
And those dreams are the only way to get u close to me
So I love going to sleep and drifting off to thoughts of u
I don't mean to be forward
But for so long I've stepped back
And watched someone else come in
Just give me the time
Not trying to impress u
But I bet u
Won't leave without being swept off your feet
All I need is one moment for us to be in love
Walking in the park and enjoying picnics
Going to the movies and sharing popcorn
As I sit and stare at the big screen wondering
"When did life get this good?"
All these things I only hope and wish and dream
But then awaken and nothing's as it seems
So I wait for the night to come
For my chance to love u all over again

I Wanna

Like the sun that melts the snow
Let me be the one that melts your heart
Let me be the one to lie next to u
When u need a comforter, let me be there
I wanna write a love poem about u
One that only u and I can relate to
I wanna tell u that you're beautiful and wonderful and that I love spending
time with u
I wanna do all those crazy things that people in relationships do
I wanna miss u, kiss u, caress u
I wanna leave u silly messages on your answering machine when I know u
just left my place
I wanna be the one u call on your cell phone on your way home from work
I wanna relax with u
Enjoy dinner and a movie with u
Laugh with u
Take naps with u
I wanna kiss u good nite and good mornings
Be that one to help u have a brighter day
And this isn't just a love poem
It's my heart speaking to u
And me wishing there were more I could do
Wanting u to stay close even though I know you're scared
But I'm afraid that you'll never know how it feels to have me care for u
I want us to share firsts, and seconds, and thirds, and etcetera etcetera
I wanna be that sweet in your dreams
Those peaches and its cream
I want u to feel what I mean when I say I just called to talk
I want people to see us and wonder
Knowing they could never truly understand
Let me be the one u share your dreams with
I wanna know what you're thinking and how you're feeling
And how u feel about me and how we feel about each other
I want us to share secrets and I want us to be secret
And wide open knowing that our bond can't be broken

4

By the little things in life
And if everything was that easy
I would have u next to me at this very moment
But this is reality and unlike my dreams
I'm holding this pen instead of u

Friendship

People come into our lives and for whatever reason leave lasting imprints
on our heart
It's nice to know that as fast as this world is changing and no matter how
much we ourselves change
There is still power in friendship
The basics never change and u still love the feeling of meeting someone
new
Our weight may change, we may dye our hair, or grow it, or cut it
But no matter what physical changes we may cause there's nuthing more
precious than spending hours talking with a good friend
Laughing and gossiping on the phone like school children
Or maybe enjoying dinner as u reminisce of when u first met, and first
loves, and first heart breaks
And congratulate each other on that new promotion, or that new love, or
whatever new thing comes up
As people stare out the corner of their eye thinking you must not've seen
each other in a while
If only they knew u do this every Saturday or Thursday or first of the
month or whenever u decide to do it
I'm talking about the type of friends that u put pictures of on your desk
and become nostalgic over every time u look at them
Because u know that u can never go back to that exact moment yet u know
that u make new ones everyday
U naively wish that u could go back to when u first met just to have the
opportunity of becoming friends again
I believe that a friend can be a first love
Who else are u most vulnerable and intimate with because any lover starts
off as a great friend
And sometimes people grow up and grow apart
That's just a way of life
But never forget the memories and all the good times u shared because
when it's all over that's the only thing that truly matters anyway
How could u forget the person who helped u get through your first heart
break, your first day of that new school, your first job, or your first move

And maybe they're not here anymore but they helped u get through those
important things
And maybe that was all God wanted them in your life for
But now u have new people to come and pick up where they left off
So this poem is about love lost, and love found, and love rekindled
After all, that's just what the soul needs

Crystal White

Sista

They make a statement when they come into the room
Make u….break your neck when they come into view
Make u…st st stutter when they come up and talk to u
She makes u stop and stare and then sashays off like she don't care
They be that box of chocolate on Valentine's Day
Chocolate on the outside but u don't know their heart until u take a bite
Cuz they come in all different flavors like caramel, mocha, milk chocolate
U better watch it or you'll get a sweet tooth
I speak the truth when I tell u the woman is beautiful
And wonderful, and intelligent and demands respect
This is for my sistas
The educated, sophisticated, degree in ghetto-ology ladies
That come braided, straight faded, finger wavin
She's high-class ain't takin no trash
Respects her man like only a true sista can
Much love to the ones raised on the street
Those type sistas are hard to defeat
Cuz they talk the talk and walk to the beat
She comes thuggin, straight lovin to rock the cords like one of the boys
But don't get it twisted she can be Miss. Mrs.
With her Capri jeans and burgundy weave
My sista ages gracefully
This woman has been strong for so long
It would be wrong to disown her
Don't get offended I'm just expressing my opinion
Giving props to the single women, holdin it down women, takin care of
they fam women
Man, u better respect this woman
She's not your average nine to five woman
She's your extra ordinary twenty-four hours, seven days a week, 365 a
year
Sista
Nod your head if u know what I mean
This for my black sista; the queen

Way of Life

The evolution of man is an interesting concept
Our environment and social actions causes us to change
Take a baby for instance
When he's hungry, hurting, scared…
He cries
He knows that when he does
Someone will be there to take care of him
As the baby grows older and becomes a child
He's more aware of the people around him
Mother and father have taught him some of life's most valuable lessons
U know, like how to share and be nice to others
So when his friend falls down, he helps him up
And when he has two and his friend has none
Well, now they both have one
See mother and father love him very much
'Cause they buy him toys and clothes and food and stuff like that
And every night before she goes to bed
They tell her how much they love their "Baby Girl."
Then as she grows older and more able to understand
She wonders why mother and father aren't together anymore
And why hasn't she seen him in a while
U know she misses being called "Baby Girl" because…
That was her name
So maybe mother and father were wrong about some things
Because she tried to share but people kept taking it all
And when she tried to help her friend up
Well, she pushed her back down
Then as she goes on to become a young woman
She realizes things aren't quite the same
Guys are beginning to look at her now
And what to do
Maybe if father was here he could…
Well, anyway
(Don't get me wrong mother did a darn good job)
So life continues to exist

9

And the more it hurts
The more she holds it inside
'Cause she realizes she's not a baby anymore
And mother and father haven't been too correct on this love thing after all
Sometimes though, she wishes they were both here to hold her hand to
leap over life's puddles
So now when he's hungry, hurting, scared…
She cries … but to himself
Because pain has become a way of life
In our evolving society
Lies have become social topics
And friends are just a figure of speech
Mothers and fathers are things of the past
Love?
Well, they believe they lost that somewhere.

A.E.G.

I'm sittin here wanting to call u so bad
Wanting to see u so bad
Wanting to get to know u so bad
And as bad as I wanna say and do all these things
Something keeps reminding me that it's only temporary
I wish this story line could be written for the next scene
But we're already on the finale
And they're canceling your character
So I'm wishing I could go back and write u into the script
Even though I know I missed the deadline and it's too late now
And now these re-runs just don't seem good enuff
It's like I've seen them over and over until I know them by heart and
although it was good entertainment back then … I'm glad it got cancelled
So I wanna try and start a new series with u as the star
I don't know how far it'll go
But no show lasts forever
Right?
Or maybe this is just part one and I have to await the sequel
Which *can* be better no matter what "they" say
But who are they anyway to say how I feel
Maybe I could just be an extra
Hey, I mean, they get perks too
And sometimes they rise up and get their spot in the limelight
Even as I'm writing this I'm wishing I could talk to u
Even as I'm writing this I'm wishing for a better way to express it
And I'm wondering why it took me so long to tune in to your station
Only to find out I'm coming in on the last season
But I guess I'll alwayz have those re-runs to watch…

CRY OF A CHILD

Born of a pure heart and a pure mind
We as children are taught hatred and bigotry
What is race but a color
What are our thoughts but the things that separate us
Born of a pure heart and a pure mind
U as parents teach us things that can make or break us
U punish me for smoking
When I seen u and daddy roll that joint
We as people have allowed our world to become corrupt and unjust
Setting morals and beliefs on a shelf to rot and rust
In a world where women do the same as men
And blacks the same as whites
There's still a superior sex and race
Children tend to do what parent's do
And we're the ones punished
For their teaching and upbringing
Born of a pure heart and a pure mind
We as children are corrupted in a day's time
Where parents don't know what's goin' on
In their own homes
Her body is robbed of innocence at the young age of five
By someone's dirty hands begging for a good time
The mixed emotions not knowing right from wrong
Robbed--
Of innocence
So the days to come are memories of past things undone
But everyday someone robs us
And I don't know what I did so wrong to make them hate me
Born of a pure heart and a pure mind
As children we ourselves must find
A way out of this destruction
Causing us to lean to our own thoughts
Living in a world of the unknown
Where we are judged and misunderstood
Searching our souls trying to find what's within . . .
But do we really know

Born of a pure heart and a pure mind
We are exposed to an atmosphere of deception
As our lives become in vain
We are plagued with rare diseases
But no one knows the cure
Is there one, or are we too ignorant to find it
Of course not 'cause we know how to make bombs out of household
goods
Born of a pure heart and a pure mind
Pride and greed have begun to run our lives
And our minds become deceived
Falling for every man-made trap
Many being the ones we've dug ourselves
Born of a pure heart and a pure mind
Living in a world of the unknown
Supposedly advanced
But what have we really come to
Increasing technology
Results in decreasing common sense
So I become secluded
U taught me everything, except how to be sociable
Born of a pure heart and a pure mind
When my brothers walk the street u lock the door
Or hold your purse closer; maybe even walk a little faster
Now them other cats are the ones blowin up buildings
And killin our innocent children
Did ya ever think of that?
Living in a world of the unknown
When my sisters speak to u they change their vocals
Instead of "ain't" it's "is not" or "are not"
"They are" instead of "they"
"We were" instead of "we be"
Born of a pure heart and a pure mind
Our differences should bring us together
'Cause our knowledge is the only thing that separates us
Black, White, Hispanic, Puerto Rican
We breathe the same air and fear the same things

Maybe my skin is darker or yours is lighter
My world is cloudy, yours is brighter
That's what they tell me
But your blood is the same color as mine
And we bleed fear
So what shade is that
'Cause fear don't have no color
Living in a world of the unknown
Physical bruises eventually heal
Emotional ones permanently scar
As I watch a man beat my mother
"The baby won't come out, she'll only die."
Too young to understand or make a difference
I could only cry
She was born on a beautiful summer day
But the doctors said she was sick . . .
And living in our world of the unknown
He started abusing his girlfriend of six months
I guess the alcohol and drugs and painful memories had him twisted
'Cause we're invincible right
Too young to die
Born of a pure heart and a pure mind
Where we're allowed to err
And forgiveness shall come thereafter
But how can we when the pain is too much to bear
Who do I talk to when no one's there
Apologies accepted
Friendships rejected
Born of a pure heart and a pure mind
They say we're growing up too fast
But our knowledge is astounding
How fast we grow up
Only to get here and wish we could go back
Keep thinking of the playground
Where we used to swing
Dreaming big dreams
Of how we were gonna be movie stars and drive fancy cars

Be doctors, lawyers,
Even veterinarians--
We were gonna make it--
The age of innocence
When the world was in the palm of our hands
And we could do anything and be anything
Then one day I woke up and looked around
And those same friends that I grew up with
And shared my aspirations with . . .
Grew up without me
And it's all gone too soon
'Cause she chose to lose
That precious gift that God had given her
At that age where she should've been shopping for clothes and nail polish
But instead she was at the pharmacy...
What ever happened to hopscotch and dodge ball
And mom dropping us off at the mall
And we're born of a pure heart and a pure mind
That evidently went out of style
'Cause we quit going to the mall and playing dodge ball
Our nights were spent in pharmacies and gas stations
Shopping for liquor and cigarettes and condoms and pregnancy tests
(Trying not to get caught)
I don't mean to alarm anyone
But don't u think we're too young
To be growing up so fast
It's ironic how u increase our economic status
While socially we're going down hill
So the weight of your mishaps is put on us
The children, are screaming out to u
Singing the song of an unwed, pregnant, teenage mother
Emotionally deprived little boy; alcohol's his only friend
Can't u feel the beat or hear the melody
Are u one with the tune
We're all crying out for help from u
You're our parents
Isn't there something u can do

15

U make us believe that u can heal anything
But what about a hurting soul
Or a pleading heart
Band-Aid can't cure that
Born of a pure heart and a pure mind
We as children watch ourselves prepare an early grave
Grace be with the souls lost and the one's yet to save
'Cause they no longer call us youth
But murderers, felons, juveniles, delinquents
Our kid's mug shots and murder scenes
Are on the cover of every newspaper and magazine
The thing that gets me
Is politicians blame the radio and the TV
But the big screen don't raise our babies
(That's what they were)
That is if parents are doing their jobs
And I'm not trying to knock them
But something needs to be said
'Cause too many of our young people are ending up dead
And visions of Oklahoma just keep replaying in my head
The children are our future
But what's in our future for the children
Too many school killings
Abusive parents
Living in a world of the unknown
Where I'm not old enuff to make my own decisions
But I'm strong enuff to deal with this emotional strain
It's hard for me to come home and you're not there,
To live up to your standards, but what about mine…
Am I too young to decide?
Born of a pure heart and a pure mind
So much goin' on these days
I could lose mine
U as parents send us to be taught,
Never ask about our teaching
And try to punish me for the grades I'm bringing
Could a baby learn to walk if no one teaches him

Eventually, but mentally he'd be scarred
The pain of nobody to care
For his tiny body, fragile and bare
So he grows up in this place we call world
And treats u not as his biological
Just someone standing there
And living in our world of the unknown
We blame everything but the one's who brought him here
Born of a pure heart and a pure mind
Hear our cry
Our heart bleeds for affection
Tongues plead for praise
Can u feel our pain
I wish u could
Living in my world of the unknown
Why do my brothers kill each other
Advanced in the world
But not in our hearts
Drawn together, yet so far apart
Born of my mother's womb
Brought up by this system
And a society that woke up a little too late
To smell the coffee
Guess this nation better switch brands
'Cause I don't want my life in no teen-ager's hands
Living by their rules
Screwed by mysterious diseases
Scratched by parents' mistakes
Pain, too deep for them to feel
Crying for my bleeding heart
Screaming because of our ignorance
Is this hittin u like it's hittin me?
'Cause for the life of me I can't understand
How I got this gun in my hand
Why u want to take the innocence
From our children
They put metal detectors and security guards in my schools

Crystal White

Because we're supposed to be the violent ones
Now on the flip side of the track
Those guys have pipe bombs and shot guns
Don't think your school's immune
When we abide by the same rules
They took prayer out of them
And all hell broke loose
They say fighting's not the answer
But when a push leads to a shove
What's my alternative?
We've been screaming to u for years
For someone who understands
But u wouldn't listen
Now you're reminiscing
Of days of young
But now I got this gun…
And everything's silent
Nobody knew I was violent
Now everyone's askin' questions
"Why? How? When?
We don't understand."
But it's not the videos or the movies
It's your inability
To love me
'Cause I just can't take it no more
Now are u listening
How we got over
Or how we're trying to overcome
Born—
Of a pure heart and a pure mind

Alton

As children we grow up not knowing what we're gonna be
Or half the time not even knowing what we wanna be
I never knew what my brother wanted to be
Or even what I wanted him to be
I thought that he'd make a good football player
Maybe go off to college and play for the Razorbacks
But, then again, he was awful skinny in those days
So maybe he would just go to college and get him a nice job somewhere
I don't even know what he was good at except getting on my nerves
He thinks he's funny so maybe he would've tried to be a comedian
I remember the day he left
I was sad … a little
But then I felt relieved cuz I no longer had to wash his dirty clothes, or
clean the kitchen after him, or close the shower curtain after he's done
(because an open shower curtain just drives me insane)
Then he was gone and I missed him
He would call me sometimes late at night just to ask me how to pass this
level on this game
And he gave me like twenty-five or fifty bucks for my graduation
Which I thought was so cool cuz I was alwayz the one to give him money
The one thing that I will remember most is the year we were both at home
at the same time
And every time I came in my room he was there
I rented us a movie and he lay on the floor and watched it while I fell
asleep in the bed
He kept waking me up during the action scenes (cuz the TV was so loud
and he was yelling)
But I didn't mind
I guess he started to sense my curiosity of his overwhelming presence
because he said
"C" (that's what he calls me) I bet u wanna know why I'm in your room
all the time
I said "yeah"
And he said it's because I miss u. I miss my little sister
I told him I missed him too and that was the end of that
Although he annoys me I often go out of my way to see him

He's my brother
So I found out he was a cook and I was thinking that's not one of those
cool jobs they show on television
But then he was over in Italy winning all these awards and medals and big
trophies
Traveling back to the states for competition which he won a bronze medal
out of like hundreds
I saw the passion in his eyes when he talked about cooking
U know he alwayz thought he was a chef anyway
Making us egg and cheese omelets and Hamburger Helper
So now when people ask me what he does
I proudly tell them he is a cook in the Army and he loves it
I can't think of anything better for him to do
I know my brother is a competitor
And I can't think of anyone else I'd rather have fighting for me
I love u
May God bless u and bring u home safe

Keepin it Real

Why is it that some people think u have to write about something profound
to be heard
Cuz sometimes all I have is love poems
And who wants to hear that
Maybe I should write about a bird or a tree
Or the bird in the tree that always flies away from me
And I don't know why
Maybe cuz when I was younger we used to try and catch 'em in one of
those old milk crates
We never could though cuz it would alwayz fly away too quickly when it
came to eat the bread
So my mom bought us parakeets instead
Cuz they were supposed to be caged
But we ran out of bird food so they died
She forgot to feed my gold fish too…and it died
Maybe that's why we could never get a dog
Back in the days when life was fun
And we were too young to understand what money was
We just knew that those money trees didn't grow in our back yards
So I guess we were poor when I was younger
But I thought everyone shopped at Payless
I just figured we got there after everyone else bought all the Nike's and
stuff
So we had to get those imitation Jordan's
I don't know why those kids laughed…cuz I really could jump higher
We never lived in the projects though
Just in bad neighborhoods with barred windows and double bolted doors
We wasn't bad either
We just ran from the cops for fun
Or maybe I wanna write a poem about stealing from the gas station
But it wouldn't be interesting cuz it was only a couple Now-N-Later's and
Blow Pops and Jolly Rancher's…
And we never got caught
So it didn't matter
Except that one time when my brother tried to get big time and steal those
baseball cards

Now that I think about it…one time they stole food from the grocery store
That doesn't count either cuz we were hungry
And at that time I'd probably rat my brother out my own self
But my mom made too much money for food stamps
So most times we ate fried bologna and cheerios
And even if u weren't poor u still couldn't resist some fried bologna with mustard
We didn't stay in the projects either
Cuz actually, we lived in the house across the street
And that's not considered the projects
It's the hood
And don't act like u too good
Cuz we've all been there
And u know what?
This poem isn't profound; but it's real

Love Potion

U know, I can't find one single thing to do to get u off my mind
Forget Love Potion # 9 u must've hit me with that dime
I know u think it's funny that I can sit here and write u these silly poems
Just so I can call and leave em on your phone
But I guess that's just one of the crazy things people in love do
I still can't seem to get thru to u though
I know your heart is in some place else right now
But for real, since I first met u, mine hasn't left
If I could right all those wrongs
I'd do it twice so we could sing a new song
I'm tired of waking up every morning and hearing the broken record
I can't seem to find a new one to replace it
Which sucks because the old one just doesn't play anymore
So I love u…
And sometimes that's all u need to say
Sometimes, that's all u can say
When that person seems so far away
Maybe my leaving will help me escape the pain of loving u
I guess I can't lose something that I never had
It's too bad cuz I think we would make great lovers
Then again, I know u and I took off in different directions a long time ago
I gotta quit holdin on
And just let this ship sink

Over U

I finally built up the nerve to get u out of my mind
To leave what we had behind
To look forward to the future without u
I hate to say that u made a mistake
But I gotta keep it real
I gave u all I could give
And dangit this poem isn't even about u
I can live without u
Sometimes I just feel like writing to express myself
And u were the first person that came in my head
But just like reality, this poem's moving on to someone else
Cuz in reality we rarely get what we want
Time is spent chasing dreams and things that seem so far away
But if we only took a moment to appreciate what we had
We would've realized that was all we needed
In reality, we see things in hindsight with no chance of redemption
Cuz we're supposed to learn from our mistakes but mistakes make us
build up a wall
It's so unfair then that the next person has to take the wrath over a
situation they had nuthing to do with
And in reality, this freakin poem is about u
It's been about u and everything I do has been about u
But there's no redeeming myself
So all I have left of u are memories, this pen, and this pad
This fight to try not to be mad
Maybe if I sleep one more hour
I'll escape the nightmare of life
I'll pull out that knife they used to stab me in my back
I'll right all those wrongs
But I've realized to just leave things alone
Cuz I am just one body, one mind, one soul
I can't make u love me or trust me
I can't turn your gray skies blue if u won't let me
I *CAN* stop thinking about u...
Until someone mentions your name or something reminds me of u
Then my heart feels empty

But like I said before –
This poem isn't even about u
I can live without u
I just need some time to gather my thoughts,
Pack up these feelings, and have a garage sell for the memories
Then I'll be on the next flight out
To Over U

Patriotism

Seventy one words we swore to uphold
I stood there bold with hands cuffed and a lump in my chest
This decision will affect the rest of my life
Can I deal with this strife?
What about my friends and family
Can they live without me
Or I without them
But I swore to support and defend the Constitution
Working for a resolution in a world where some don't see
The obstacles placed before me
And the sacrifices that I make every day
For their freedom to live in this great place
Fresh out of high school
Barely eighteen
Now I have my finger on this M-16
First time away from home
And I'm living alone
Sometimes in a foreign land
With the world's freedom in the palm of my hand
There's a huge weight I bare on my shoulders
Obeying the orders of my Commander in Chief and those appointed over
me
Whose weight is bigger than mine
But if u look in our eyes
U won't see fear
Because we all stood there
So u could stand here … freely
So that your kids could play in the streets
We choose to live this way
So that some day when we're old and gray
Our kids can fight not to have our freedom taken away
This is for the ones who came before us
Who had no choice
But fought the good fight and gave their life
Because they believed in what was right
Their lives are not gone in vain

Because we raised our right hand and swore to do the same
We wear the uniform that represents freedom and gets respect from so many
Some who have lost loved ones and some that realize their freedom did not come without a price
They gave their life for a day they will never see
So take a minute and be thankful for the ones overseas protecting u and me
The ones u work beside, jog beside, each lunch beside, everyday
All day … we are on watch
And when our time is up someone taps us out and picks up where we left off
Because a soldier's work is never done but there's no place we'd rather be
Than in this uniform
Defending this great country
"As I lay me down to sleep, I pray the Lord, my soldier's keep…" So help me God

Unfinished

Sometimes I sit and wonder when my break is gonna come
And ponder on why it's been takin so long
Been singin the same song
Just to different beats every other week
And if I keep this up I'm gonna be washed up
A has been with friends tellin stories of how I used to be
Cuz they knew me in the days when I could blaze a page
They ask me what happened
I guess I just lost my passion
Got tired of holdin on to hopes and dreams
It seems like everyone's out for me
I used to believe but now I just see
Every man's for himself so don't get left behind
They'll rob u blind until u have no piece of mind
I've seen it with my own eyes
Got stabbed in the back right in front of me
It's dumb of me to keep moving forward
But at the end of this tunnel there's gotta be light
I need some chance to make these wrongs right
I knew I should've turned left at the light
Gotta get back to the place I was before I lost it…
I gotta snap back to reality
Some people are like gravity
They only bring u down
The worst are friends that pretend to be down with me
But when I turn my back they're the first enemy
The first to ridicule, take a bite, chew it up, then spit at u
The fact I gave everything I had
And they still want me on my back is something that I just can't grasp
They're like vultures
Sent to eat my flesh til there's nuthing left of me
But I won't let them get the best of me
I used to write rhymes religiously
Poetry was mine
My time to unwind
Expressing feelings and thoughts

U thought that I was nuthin
That I wasn't worthy of your affection
But now you're second-guessin
Cuz I got yo' number
But never called it
U thought it…was a game
But with this pen and pad
I'm invincible
U only see this ink but u can't blot those thoughts I've placed in your head
The beat is never dead
It's only silenced; bound by the chains of those that can't feel it
It's in bondage
But don't u know u can't keep a strong poem down long
It forms from the darkest valley of your soul
And grows
Sometimes it just seems like I have a pen with no ink
No time to sit and think
Life just sidetracks me
And my hopes…are floating down the river in a boat…alone
With no place to call home
Til a kid picks 'em up and calls 'em his own
I hope she can make those dreams come true
I feel as though I failed u because they wanted me to quit
And I must admit…for a minute I did
But I can't pawn my dreams off on the next soul
To be swallowed whole
I gotta take control
Cuz nobody owes us a thing

Lies

Lies lies
They're all lies
Masking their deception
Looking in my eyes
I've heard em all before
I let u in thru the front
But u snuck out the back door
Turning my inside
Too stubborn to cry
Such is life
U live and u die
People do what they do to get by
Who am I to judge
Not holdin a grudge only makes my heart harder
So why bother to keep it real
When they're full of evil
Put trust in no man
Cuz your stone is just his sand
Easily brushed away
Await for a better day
When they can see your face
And be truthful
Lies are youthful
I gave that up
Along with trust
Cuz they all lie

The Wrong "Man"
To a really good friend

Do u believe that I can make your heart sing,
Give u things that u need,
Treat u like the queen that u are
Send u flowers when you're sad or just because I was thinking of u
U know in your mind that he don't give u the time and attention u deserve
But you're willing to stick it out and try and make it work
But if I make a mistake it's over
There's no redemption
To u I'm wicked now and u can't see how u ever fell for me in the first
place
I wish that u would face the facts
U did it and u can never take it back
But u run into the arms of someone who doesn't love u
And I trusted u with my heart even when I knew I shouldn't do that
Too late to take it back
It's already broken
And left with words unspoken
Wouldn't know what to say anyway
So if he makes u happy
(Even though I know u cry at nite)
And makes u exhale
(Though you're drowned in tears)
Then maybe that's where u should be
If you're not comfortable with me
But haven't I dried your tears or stopped them from falling
When u were depressed I was the one u were calling on the other end
Not him
Maybe I am just a friend but u never should've mixed the two
When u knew that I was feelin u
I need u to understand
Him, being a man, doesn't make him a lover
One can say anything under covers
And now that he's mistreating u
You're looking for advice from me
But I still can't see past my own pain
They say love is blind

Crystal White

But in my case …
They alwayz see

U Probably Think This Poem Is About U
Now I've dated my fair share
Not many but a few
And I've never seen the likes of u
Someone that gets to me the way that u do
After all this time u still send chills down my spine
U put butterflies in my stomach
I love it
This feeling that u give me
When we're together I'm in ecstasy
And nuthing seems to matter but your happiness
If I can make u smile then it's all worth while
If all I can do is hold u
I'll do just that to show u what u mean to me
U make me feel complete
Everyday I try to let u know that I mean these words I say
I really don't mean to be forward but u feed my mentals
Believe me, it's not sexual
I just love to lie next to ya
I try to give u your space and play it cool
But sometimes it just drives me crazy
When I can't see u or talk to u
I don't even know where this poem is going but I hope it's showing u how
I feel…
Cuz it's real
I think
U know, I'm tired of writing these love poems
Am I really in love or do I just write em cuz they sound good
Where did a poem ever get me anyway
U were feelin me way before I even thought to write u a poem
The sad thing is that who knows you're gonna be worthy of this poem a
couple years, months, or even days from now
Heck, I'll probably be regrettin it within the next hour
I'll probably stumble upon it and be mad for real
Because I wasted my time writing this poem about u
Obviously u didn't pay attention to anything I had to say
If u did, we would be together

It's okay though, cuz I'll just recycle it and use it on the next person
Ha, they would never know, and neither would u
Unless I told u to hurt your feelings because u hurt mine
But I'm way too mature for that
I just wanna write a poem about everyday life
Not about how you've made everything right and how happy I am now
that you're in my world
Let the truth be told
Regardless of what that poem says, I *will* find someone else

Time After Time
Time after time I lie awake
And notice u sleeping
Wondering what kind of dreams you're dreaming
Are they the same ones that terrorize me night after night
Or…maybe yours are filled with sugar canes and dandelions
Time after time I lie awake
So u can fall asleep
And I can feel like I'm protecting u
Like being your guardian angel
Like…I wish someone had done me
Time after time I lie awake
Wishing I was someone's everything
Cuz all those I love are everything to me
As you're lying there
I wonder are your dreams as big as mine
Because I want so much out of life
Maybe if I just knew what u were dreaming
I could…never mind
Time after time I lie awake
And appreciate the fact that you're who u are
And u accept me for who I am
It's really nice to know
That I have a place to go
When times get pretty tough
I just lie awake time after time…
Thinking

Scenario

Life? I don't know what to think
Sometimes I blink and it passes me
This world is crazy
I wish someone would come and save me
And take me somewhere to make me someone else
But I like me
I just wanna see what it would be to live another's life
Maybe someone rich and famous
Or maybe someone dirt poor and broke as ….
With no door and no hope of ever comin up
So reality would slap me in the face
And I'd realize that my place isn't that bad
There's millions who wish they had what I have
There's some old retired man in the lobby reminiscing on his life and how
times have changed
He seems happy but he's on the Psych Ward so he could be deranged
Maybe he's bipolar and in one of his manic moods
U know, one of them old dudes who could sit and talk for hours
About the way things were when he was a young boy
How they were poor
And had to walk five miles to the store
In the blizzard of '39
With his dog that was blind and missing a leg
I tell the receptionist I'll wait
Rush this man ahead
Maybe someday I'll have stories to tell
And deeper poems to write
About my life and my struggle
But nobody wants to hear u complaining and whining
Cuz we all have to hustle from time to time
Working overtime just to make that extra dime
That we never see
Committing ourselves to places that we could never be
Take the wool from over your eyes so u can see
Everybody's just tryin to get a piece of the American pie
What would u do

Steal, kill, lie
Don't say never cuz when u hit rock bottom
U just might
Take a life
So u can eat or put shoes on ur feet
When times are hard
And even harder when u got mouths to feed
It makes u wonder what u would do
If the shoe was on the other foot
So greet me when u see me on the street
Don't just look the other way
Cuz u don't know what kind of day I've had
I might be steamin mad
And u just ignited my fire
So now I'm gonna burn u
Cuz I just got laid off and my woman's due in a month or two
So I don't have time for u to look down on me
U walked right past, stared, and didn't speak
But now if I jack u I'll fit another stereotype
Of an unemployed black man who steals to support his family
Naw, that's not me
Besides, this shop across the street has a vacancy

Caught Up

I want u to get caught up in me
Cuz I am caught up in u
But I know we both have to pretend to be cool
I wanna escape in your world
Because mine gets crazy sometimes
Just maybe … we could be crazy together
But u bring out a part of me that's just free
At times when there's broken pieces
You're the part that makes it complete
And I know that sounds corny
But you get the best of me
I knew I wanted u the first moment I laid eyes on u
So now that I know u better that desire grows even stronger
How much longer do I have to wait
How much longer are we gonna pretend
That we're just friends
And if we just act natural these feelings will end
But those things u didn't want for us
Cuz u left without a trace
No goodbye, no phone call, not even a letter
Should I have known better than to pursue u
Cuz u told me u weren't good in relationships
I guess it's one of those things that we never listen to until the end
Not that I regret u in any way
Maybe our day will come when we don't have to be scared
Scared to be in love
And to be in love with the person we're in love with
Cuz when it's all said and done
We're the ones who's gonna be accountable
Not everyone else
Who said we shouldn't be together
Nobody knew how we were when we were alone
Or when we spent hours on the phone
Talking about our passions for the same thing
Just like u don't know
How badly I want to be with u

Games

Is this a game to u
Cuz if it is let me know the rules so I can play too
How is it that u can act like u can't live without me
Then turn around and be with someone else
It's funny how they alwayz show up at the right moment
Just to listen
So I lie awake wanting to talk to u
Thinking u're asleep
But u got company
So don't I feel like an idiot
So did she ask u why u still wanted to be with me
Or did u tell her that u wanted to be with her
U just rubbed that in my face too
Like I didn't mean nuthin to u
Like we didn't just spend our weekend together
So if this is a game just let me know
So I can say u won
And we can just move on
Cuz what's the point in holding on
When all we're doin is playin games

Aunt Meal

1622 Hanger St. was not just where Aunt Meal lived
It was my second home
Toni and I spent many weekends and summer vacations in that house
Aunt Meal never seemed to complain
Even when she had a house full of nieces and nephews
She just whipped up a pot of spaghetti and fed us
And if u knew Aunt Meal then u know she loved to feed people
And if u told her u didn't like a certain food she'd tell u "That's because u
haven't had mine yet."
(She was usually right)
Even if u never met Aunt Meal u loved her just from hearing her family
talk about her
But if Aunt Meal met u once she would always remember u
There are so many good things I can say about her
But Aunt Meal had too much character to be gone
So her memory lives on … in us
Aunt Jimmie … when Missy starts instigating with Bruce and Greg…
She gets it from Aunt Meal
And Ma, when I call u up and u think I've talked too long…
I get it from Aunt Meal
So just laugh…
That's what she would've wanted

40

About The Author

Crystal White is an exceptional poet who has been writing for over 10 years. She has been asked to write poems for numerous events around her community in 2003 such as Dr. Martin Luther King, Jr. birthday celebration, Women's Equality Day, and Black History Month just to name a few. Crystal was also selected to be an alternate member on the Dayton Poetry Slam Team in 2002. She has written a stage play that was performed during Black History Month. Everything she writes brings inspiration to all that hear it.